Love, Life, Grief and Joy
Review

A vulnerable memoir about living with loss, even before that loss occurs, Love, Life, Grief and Joy by Donna Jean Fletcher is a stirring and passionately penned account of resilience and relentless faith. This expanded version of an earlier memoir delves deep into the author's struggles and strategies before and after the loss of her beloved partner and fellow pastor to cancer. Cathartic for those readers who might painfully relate, and instructive for all who will face grief in the future, this deeply personal and compassionate read will linger in the heart far past the final page.

4.5 star rating

Editor, SelfPublishReview

GRIEF'S STORY; Joy Will Come
REVIEWS

Grief's Story is a touching and honest memoir of a woman, wife, and mother's experience living with her husband as he slowly succumbs to a difficult cancer diagnosis. Sharing her intimate private moments of grief and uncertainty, the author also offers a window into not only her grief but also her ultimate joy as she turns things over to God for comfort. The writing is generally clear and easy to follow.

WestBow Press

Grief's Story; Joy Will Come is truly heartbreaking, yet the ultimate comforter and healer at the same time. This teaches us all to be brave and believe that God is always there to guide and help in any way possible. No pain will last forever. Time heals a broken heart. Very beautiful plot line.

Tate Publishing

A debut memoir that looks at life before and after widowhood.

Author Fletcher/Everitt and her late husband, Garry, had ten grown children and were Salvation Army assistant pastors. Garry fell ill in March 1995, suffering from a fever, accompanied by chills and sweating. He weakened and lost weight in the months to come; in October, a lymph-node biopsy revealed cancer, and by the following May, doctors concluded that chemotherapy wasn't working and nothing else could be done. Fletcher/Everitt astutely notes that her mourning had already started by that point: "the grieving process begins during terminal illnesses. It doesn't wait until after the person dies." She and Garry returned to their Kansas hometown from Michigan, and he entered hospice care.

Even in his weakened state, he insisted on planning everything, including memorial funds, his obituary, and gifts for each family member. The memoir includes just the right details to convey what the author was going through, ranging from the awful (10 trash bags full of bloodied diapers) to the surreal (Garry recorded a message to be played at his funeral that started "Hi, Donna"). Excerpts from family newsletters, and what appears to be a journal she kept at the time, are presented in a different typeface. The author's account of the months after the funeral appropriately feels quite scattered, relying heavily on prayers and diary entries. The events of the next decade and more, however, are presented too selectively; in particular, the memoir is vague about the author's dating experiences and a broken engagement.

It also divulges next to nothing about the author's second marriage. The last quarter of the book provides a rushed tour through other losses, including the deaths of Fletcher/Everitt's father and one of her daughters. Readers may find that the subtitle's promised joy is rather hard to find amid the bereavement, although Fletcher/Everitt does express gratitude for her blessings—a husband, many grandchildren, a new puppy—in a final prayer. (Includes black-and-white family photographs.)

A tragic but vividly detailed narrative.

Kirkus Indie, Kirkus Media LLC,

Grief's Story, Joy will Come

LOVE, LIFE, GRIEF AND JOY

DONNA JEAN FLETCHER

Grief's Story; Joy Will Come
Expanded Edition

Copyright © 2022 Donna Jean Fletcher

All rights reserved. No part of this book may be reproduced, stored, or transmitted by any means—whether auditory, graphic, mechanical, or electronic—without written permission of both publisher and author, except in the case of brief excerpts used in critical articles and reviews. Unauthorized reproduction of any part of this work is illegal and is punishable by law.

ISBN: 978-1-63950-096-3 (sc)
ISBN: 978-1-63950-097-0 (e)

The views expressed in this work are solely those of the author and do not necessarily reflect the views of the publisher, and the publisher hereby disclaims any responsibility for them.

Writers Apex

Gateway Towards Success

8063 MADISON AVE #1252
Indianapolis, IN 46227
+13176596889
www.writersapex.com

"I tell you the truth,
You will weep and mourn
While the world rejoices,
You will grieve,
But your grief
Will turn to joy".

John 16:20, NIV

CONTENTS

Preface xi

Chapter 1   Garry 1

Chapter 2   Keep Trying 7

Chapter 3   Preparing 15

Chapter 4   Living Life 23

Chapter 5   Final Days 35

Chapter 6   Good-Byes 43

Chapter 7   Life After Death 51

Chapter 8   Memorial Windows 63

Chapter 9   Dealing With Grief 67

Chapter 10 Dating 75

Chapter 11 Mom 79

Chapter 12 Moving Forward 83

Chapter 13 Debbie 87

Chapter 14 Larry 99

Chapter 15 Changes 109

Chapter 16 Moving On 117

Chapter 17 Memories 121

PREFACE

My first book, *Grief's Story Joy will Come,* was written to help me traverse through my grief and to give others encouragement while dealing with their particular trials. At readers' requests, I expanded that story. This is the finished product.

A quote by Ted Dekker says, "A good story is a series of events involving worthy characters who change because of those events." Writing, rewriting and editing *Love, Life, Grief and Joy* brought tears of pain and joy flowing onto the keyboard.

This story was to be about those in it. But I am surprised to find that it is about me. God, and each of these people and events, have brought about changes in me.

I learned that, at times, I have put my faith in the storms bombarding me and the power they had over me. Faith should be in the Maker of life, Jesus Christ. My prayer for you is to see bits of your life and how to get through any situation with His strength.

Garrett W. Fletcher

CHAPTER 1

GARRY

In March 1995, my husband, Garry Fletcher, began running fevers in the late afternoons and through the nights. The chills and profuse sweating went along with these. At six feet two inches, he weighed three hundred and eight pounds.

He went to a doctor in the small town where we were serving as assistant pastors for The Salvation Army. The doctor seemed unable to believe what Garry said had been happening. We found that many times, when doctors have medical personnel as patients, they think that the patient is second guessing their diagnosis. But whatever the reason, he found nothing and didn't do any follow up.

Since he had worked in the medical field as a physician's assistant for thirty years, Garry had some tests run on his own. The health department found no AIDS, TB, or any other prevalent diseases of the day. He started losing weight and had less energy, patience, and no "oomph" at all.

In September, we went to another town with a large hospital and clinic. On moving day, he couldn't carry anything but the really light things. Even that was hard for him because our apartment was on the second floor.

~~~

Garry was the shopper of our family; he loved to shop. It did not matter if it was a grocery store, thrift store, or fancy clothing store. He even did the monthly sanitary run for me and six teenage girls. Many times, I would stay in the car and read while he shopped.

In October, he came rushing out of the grocery store. His teeth were chattering from fever. He asked me if I would drive him to the hospital. At the emergency room, they suggested we go to the drop-in clinic in the hospital. I almost had to drag him along, but we finally got to the clinic department. (A wheelchair would have been a good idea.)

The clinic doctor asked Garry when the fever had started. His answer was, "Last March." The doctor about had a fit. He said, "And you waited until twenty minutes before we close to come to the clinic?" Garry's response was that he was sorry, and he could come back tomorrow. The doctor said, "No way... We've got you here now. We are going to find out what is going on."

They started running test after test and ended up doing a biopsy of his lymph glands. We both felt that we knew what was wrong with him. At the library, we copied everything we found on cancer. No one had told us, but we knew he was dying. He had already lost about a hundred pounds.

~~~

The Friday before Thanksgiving, his mom, brother, and sister came to visit us. His sister's arriving comment was, "Your heathen sister is here to see you."

The church was having a lady's outing that night. Since his family was with him, I attended so they could have some "alone" time with him.

While I was sitting in a hot tub in the snow, eating snacks, then watching the "Santa Clause" movie, the doctor called Garry and told him he had cancer. When I think about how I was enjoying myself when he got that call, I become very upset. I should have been with him instead of having fun while he was getting this life shattering news.

Why wasn't I with him? I am very glad that his family was there. I definitely would not have wanted him to be alone.

~~~

Garry was to start chemotherapy on December fourth. After church, the day before his first treatment, I insisted we get our picture taken at K-mart. We ended up waiting three hours before they got to us. Everyone in town must have been getting Christmas portraits done that day.

Garry was so tired. He didn't want to keep waiting, but I felt we could not leave. For his family, we needed to do this before chemotherapy started. I didn't know how right I was, but the pictures showed it. He only looked a little like himself. (He'd lost a lot of weight and he had dark circles under his eyes.)

Our favorite picture was one Garry saw on the monitor. He asked the photographer to take it. He was facing me with his hand on my shoulder. We were looking at each other. Because it wasn't posed and was so natural, everyone wanted that picture. It hung on my gallery wall for many years.

Garry & Donna Fletcher

CHAPTER 2

KEEP TRYING

During his first round of chemo, I visited him three or four times a day. We celebrated our twentieth anniversary at the hospital. Ten days later, I ended up being pushed into his hospital room in a wheelchair by one of the emergency room staff. I had fallen on the ice in a parking lot and had a badly sprained ankle. I did the rest of the visits for that round of chemo on crutches.

Since we worked together, I felt I needed to carry his workload and my own. Between working, hospital visits and caring for him at home, I was exhausted.

He was in the hospital a week, home two, then back again. After three rounds of treatments, more tests were completed. The cancer was still growing.

~~~

Feeling claustrophobic at home was a new feeling for me, since we had always lived in large houses. Now, with all of our children grown, we were living in an efficiency apartment.

We hated that he had to climb thirteen steps to our place. I suggested we move somewhere with no stairs. He said no. I didn't understand why. Later I realized that the thought of moving again was unbearable to him.

Each evening, he would lie on the couch with his head on my lap and sleep. I didn't want to move any part of my body because I didn't want to wake him.

I would look at him for hours, seeing a man I didn't know. Before dad died, mom said she felt like she was living with a stranger. Now I understood.

~~~

Garry's belly used to be very prominent. Since he lost it, his pants no longer fit. He takes them off without loosening the belt. While walking, they fall down. Cutting down his belt just isn't doing the trick. So we thought outside the box. It was time for suspenders. To make it fun, I bought every color they had in the store.

~~~

The apartment across the hall became available. It was almost twice the size of ours and only forty-five dollars more a month. I told him I would like to move into it. He reluctantly agreed. Some church people came and helped.

It bothered him he was not helping, so he picked up four books. Carrying them the few steps across the hall just exhausted him. His earthly vessel was defiantly failing him.

~~~

They changed his chemo treatment. He took pills at home, then the hospital for twenty-four hours each time. After several rounds, the tests showed no measurable results.

Because of chemotherapy, he became weaker, lost weight from throwing up, and lost all his body's hair, even his eyelashes. I may have thought that he didn't look like himself before, but now he looks like a hairless, homeless, ninety-year-old guy.

He has had facial hair since 1976. That year, he was working TDY in Chicago for the Federal Prison. The kids and I were in Kansas. I went to pick him up at the train station in Kansas City.

He had told me he would meet me in the parking lot. Not seeing him, I parked. A nice looking man in a winter coat and full beard opened my car door. My response was "Can I help you?" He said "I sure hope so."

While in Chicago, he had grown a full beard. This was during the first year of our marriage. He only shaved once after that because our three-year-old wouldn't have anything to do with him. Her daddy had hair on his face, so he never shaved again.

~~~

March 1996, a friend of his in Kansas died of cancer. He wanted to attend the funeral, but had no strength. I don't think he could manage it emotionally. Besides, he had to go for another round of chemo.

~~~

He finished that round on the Thursday before Easter. We were planning to visit his sister. She could no longer say that she was his "heathen sister." She had accepted Jesus as her Savior and would become a church member on Easter Sunday. He told her that his sickness was worth it if it brought her to Christ.

He was to hold a flag for the ceremony, but he was too weak. This was the first time ever that he wanted me to drive while on a trip.

~~~

Later that month, I was watching television after he went to bed. I cried and cried because someone in the movie died of cancer. Of course, I was crying for my husband, our lost future, and for myself.

I was grieving. I didn't know that the grieving process begins during the terminal illness. It doesn't wait until after the person dies. It was hard getting control, but I had to. I didn't want to explain why I'd been crying.

~~~

Spring 1996, he continues to run the soup kitchen, go to the office every day, and even preach sometimes. All the offices are on the second floor, straight up, seventeen steps. He stands at the bottom and hangs onto the rail. Then he takes a couple of steps, stops, rests, then takes a few more steps, till he gets to the top. We have offered moving his office downstairs, but he refused. He doesn't want to cause problems or give up.

~~~

People at work and church members visit and pray with us and for us. We've only been here a short time, yet they care.

Neighbors in our apartment building are always asking about him. One of them brought him a pewter guardian angel pin. He has been wearing it to work.

~~~

We have always enjoyed eating out. Now he can only eat a couple of bites before throwing up. Eating at home, makes him feel worse because of the smells. He says they make his belly sick. Through the years, he has done the cooking for our family. Since he no longer can, it makes his heart sick. We even had a sign in our kitchen that read, "Garry's Kitchen."

~~~

In May, the doctor said nothing more could be done. Garry asked if we should move back home. The doctor's reply was, "I think that would be the best. You can have time with your children. You probably have less than six months to live." Back at the church, we told the pastor we would be leaving.

~~~

Garry's last sermon there started with him leaning against the pulpit and ended with him sitting in a chair. It was hard to hear him, even with the microphone, because his voice was growing weak along with the rest of his body.

His voice used to be as big and hardy as he was. Even when he whispered, everyone around him could hear. After work, to excite the little ones, he would yell, "Shut up" at the door. They would come running. To find him in a store, I would listen for his voice. He would be talking to someone, anyone, a friend, acquaintance or stranger.

~~~

We stopped at his mom's house in Illinois on our way back to Kansas. When she opened the door, I was standing behind him. She looked at him and started slamming the door until she saw me. She did not recognize her own son, even though she had just seen him a few weeks' prior. I didn't realize that it was as hard on her as it was on me.

It made me realize that when dealing with grief, each person is coming from a unique vantage point. The relationship and memories we have with the person will cause us to grieve in our own individual way. One person's illness or death will cause unique feelings in every person who knows them.

It makes sense. Two people never relate the same. Unfortunately, there isn't a guide book telling us how to feel, or deal with death and grief.

CHAPTER 3

PREPARING

After I drove Garry to my mother's house in Kansas, and I went back to Michigan, I worked another week while packing up the apartment. One of my sons-in-law and Garry's sister came and helped me pack the U-Haul and move home.

We put the furniture in storage and moved to Mom's. We owned a home here, but rented it while out of state. We would have loved to live there. But we couldn't kick out our grand-kids, daughter and her husband who were living there. Besides, thinking about Mom with my dad, I didn't think I wanted him to die in the house we got married in.

~~~

Staying at my mom's is wonderful and difficult because Dad had died in the living room four years ago. She had refused hospice care because she didn't want strangers in her home. Now, Garry wants hospice services, but we are not sure how Mom will handle it. Of course, she agreed to it, but I feel we are imposing on her privacy.

~~~

Garry wants me to work. There is not a job available with our church in this town. A position elsewhere would mean an hour's drive each way, and I need to be available for him.

How can I leave him alone while I look for work? I don't want Mom to have to take care of him. Our doctor says it would be better for both of us if we continued our life as usual. (Yeah right...) I haven't figured out how we are supposed to do that. Nothing is the same.

~~~

Garry spends lots of time in bed. He uses a wheeled walker to get to the bathroom. Mom had a ramp put on her house when Dad was sick, so we can take Garry in Dad's wheelchair when he has to leave the house.

Hospice services are really great. They have a nurse come and visit every couple of days. Mom seems fine with it, so I should not have been concerned.

~~~

In July, we went to Kansas City with my mom and sister to one of his favorite restaurants. Garry ate, but he threw up three times in the parking lot. Every time he eats, he throws up. He even does it sometimes when he doesn't eat.

~~~

Garry did a lot of thinking while laying in that bed. One day that July, while I was job hunting, he called the funeral home and had an undertaker come to Mom's house. He had wanted to drive himself to see the caskets and pick his own, but he couldn't drive anymore, so he chose from a catalog.

They took care of all the funeral and burial plans. He had everything arranged. Arriving home, he told me what I would have to do after his death. (Like death certificates needed to collect insurance, and all the other "business stuff.") It was difficult to have him lay out details for his funeral. But he was trying to save me from anguish.

~~~

July thirteenth, we had a family picnic at the park. We all wore T-shirts with a picture of either Garry or my dad on them. Dad's said, 'Dunlap Gang' and Garry's read 'Fletcher Clan'. Everyone came. His family all drove from the Chicago area. The people who had not seen him since he got sick didn't recognize him. How could they?

It was a wonderful time of memories and laughter.

~~~

It was necessary to buy my first cell phone so I could be reached any time. I got a job as a secretary at a mechanical company. I found a rental house because Garry didn't want to die in Mom's house. It would be too hard for her. He is still thinking of others first.

~~~

While at the rental, two Mormons came to the door. I told them I was just moving in. They asked, "Is there anything we can do to help." My answer was, "If you are serious, meet me tomorrow at 9:00 a.m."

They came and brought others. The day was spent loading and unloading the U-Haul. As always, God provided (Even from very unexpected sources.)

~~~

Mom, Garry, and I stopped at a yard sale after his doctor's appointment. He even got out of the car.

We bought him some shirts because his were all so big on him. The lady insisted he buy a winter coat, too. Something was bothering him. When we got in the car, he said he felt he had to buy the coat. He couldn't tell her he knew he would be dead before winter.

With cancer and death bombarding him all the time, how can he deal with it and still have such a joyous spirit? The obvious answer is that the Holy Spirit is giving him the grace and peace he needs to manage it all.

~~~

My new job is boring me. It doesn't keep me busy enough. So many things are happening at home. I suggested they shorten my hours, but they say that they need someone to answer the phones and take care of walk-in customers.

They allow me to do personal things when the office is slow. Correspondence college courses through our church education department and playing Super Tetris on the company computer became my past times. I spend my lunch hours at home with Garry.

~~~

The kids would take turns staying with him while I worked. My eldest daughter came from New Mexico and spent a month. The US Army released his son for three weeks' compassionate leave after verification by the American Red Cross. God worked it all out. Again.

The grand-kids brought him pictures they had colored. I taped them up on his oxygen tanks so he could see them.

~~~

One day, the local minister came over. He wanted Garry to write or tape a 'final sermon' for the church, something telling everyone what it was like knowing that you were dying. It was to be his last word to them.

I didn't like the idea. He was sick, weak, and dying. His voice was barely audible. My impression was, he didn't have the stamina to do what they wanted.

~~~

One of our daughters had twin girls in August. They were both less than five pounds. Their parents would bring one at a time to visit. In the carrier placed beside his bed, Garry could see them.

He loved to watch them. He had me lay them in bed with him. One day he tried to kiss the eldest one on her head while she was lying on his chest. He couldn't raise his head. I lifted her so he could give her his kiss. I felt like he was "giving the blessing" like they did in the Old Testament times.

~~~

At work, I wrote a family newsletter every few weeks. They let me copy and prepare it for mailing too. It went to more than three hundred people across the country.

~~

Garry and the minister have been talking about setting up a memorial fund. Our church has simple, colored glass windows. Garry checked with the stained-glass business owner and they planned what he would like done. He wants stained glass windows over the main entrance doors. One window will have the lion and the lamb lying down together. With enough donations, the second window will be The Salvation Army crest and a pair of doves.

~~~

Garry began talking to me about what I was to do with the insurance money; pay bills, then put some in the credit union and leave it there. They have a special program. Whatever you have in your savings on your fifty-fifth birthday (still more than seven years away for me) that amount will be doubled on death. Then the kids will have burial money for me. My life insurance was through his work. They canceled it when he retired.

He wanted some of the tithe money from his life insurance to be given to Catholic Social Service and hospice because of their help and devotion during his illness. The balance was to be used for the stained-glass window fund for church. Any leftover should be used to fill other needs at the church.

He had planned everything. Not wanting flowers at the funeral, he preferred people to give memorials to the stained-glass window fund or to the local Hospice.

~~~

In mid-August, he had me type his obituary to check the information out. He felt that by helping me do all this; it would be easier later. But it was still hard. One good thing, I wouldn't forget what he wanted in it.

~~~

Excerpts from:

FLETCHER FAMILY NEWS Vol. 2

MEDICAL UPDATE: GARRY FLETCHER (GRANDPA TO MOST OF YOU YOUNG'UNS)

Garry is being seen by hospice regularly. He has oxygen at home to help him feel better. He cannot keep down solid food, so he drinks instant breakfast and Ensure and eats soft stuff like eggs, Jell-O and pudding.

At the last report, he weighs one hundred and sixty pounds. His mind is still functioning. When commenting on his weight, he used one of his famous 'one liners'. "I had to get rid of the weight so I can get into Heaven . . . Everyone knows the door to Heaven is a narrow one."

The highlight of his day is when the mailman comes. The problem is, just moving, all he gets is junk mail. His best time of the day is late afternoons and early evening. We encourage visitors to come over during these hours.

CHAPTER 4

LIVING LIFE

He can no longer eat food of any kind. He has been drinking Ensure, but now he can't keep that down either. The doctor suggested Carnation Instant Breakfast mixed with ice cream. It sounds great to me. Hurray! He likes it, and so do I.

Nothing fits him anymore. His wedding ring keeps falling off his finger. He asked me to put it away.

His hair has grown back. It is all white now. The top is still bald, like always. He said that he was hoping for a full head of hair. His beard is white as snow.

He had me take him to Wal-mart in Dad's wheelchair after his doctor's appointment. He wanted to buy some coloring for it. We got the coloring, but he is too tired for me to color it.

Guess what? The ice-cream instant breakfast didn't last very long. Now, he can't stand chocolate, and he says there is something wrong with the vanilla. He is trying to take nourishment, though. Praise God.

~~~

In late August, he decided he wanted to go for a ride. I tried to talk him out of it, as there was no one to help me put him into the van, and it was late. Besides that, it was pouring down rain. I gave in, put him in the wheelchair, wheeled him to the porch, and helped him get down the six steps. This house doesn't have a ramp like Mom's does.

I pulled the van to the steps and opened the door. When I tried to get him in, I only managed to get his top half across the seat. He was lying on his stomach with his long legs and feet still hanging out. It took a lot of finagling, since my height is only five feet one and a half inch. But I finally got him into a sitting position and out of the rain.

He wanted a cherry-limeade from Sonic. They were closed, but the employees were still cleaning up. I asked the girl to please come out and talk to me. My smallest bill was a ten, so I held it to her and asked for the drink.

She said that they had already closed out the register so they didn't have change. I told her I didn't care and that she could have the ten. She took one look at him, then got him the Route 44 size, the biggest they make. She told me to keep my money.

Driving and trying to help him with the large cup in his lap was a fiasco. He couldn't hold it in his hands, so I put it between his legs on the seat. I was trying to get his mouth to the straw when he almost fell out of the seat. I tried to lift it up, but that was impossible while driving.

Maybe I was not driving my best because a cop stopped me. Jumping out, I realized I had no jacket or shoes, and it was still raining. He may have thought that I was high on something. I tried to explain the situation to him. He probably thought I couldn't make up that story. He let me go without even looking at Garry or checking my driver's license.

When I got back in, Garry did not realize what had happened. He stated he wanted to go downtown and check out Buffalo Bill Days, an annual festival in our hometown. He used to be part of this celebration when he was younger in the Jaycees. Mom had told him it was happening this month. I tried to explain that it was already over for this year, but he insisted we go. Of course, I drove toward town for him.

He asked why I had turned the corner. I told him I was taking him downtown. He informed me we had already been there, and it was okay to take him home now.

I pulled up to the house. The rain was coming down, and the porch still had those steps. It was easier pulling him down out of the van than it had been pushing him into it. I prayed that with God's help, and maybe a little help from Garry, we would make it up the steps.

By the time I got him inside and into bed with dry clothes, I was so past ready for bed myself. Things that we take for granted, like a comfortable bed, take on a whole new meaning when exhaustion hits.

~~~

An excerpt from:

FLETCHER FAMILY NEWS Vol. 3
GRANDPA GARRY

Garry is on a full liquid diet now. A hospital bed in the archway between the dining room and living room allows him to be 'in the swing' of things. He has a machine that makes oxygen for him. One granddaughter saw it and stated he is "Being a doctor today."

He is writing the sermon he will tape for the church congregation to hear sometime in the future.

For those of you who weigh more than one hundred and fifty pounds, Garry now weighs less than you do.

~~~

Labor Day, September second, was coming up soon. Garry decided we needed to have a shindig. He and the kids planned a

"Thanksgiving" picnic. With his help, I went through his personal things and made up bags of goodies as early Christmas presents for each member of the family. With ten kids, in-laws, and twenty-four grandchildren, that was quite a feat.

He gave me his wedding ring and the first tie tack I had ever bought him. He told me to give the ring to my next husband. On our tenth anniversary, we had reaffirmed our wedding vows and exchanged rings. He gave his anniversary ring to our first grandson.

Such a special time, going through personal things and picking gifts for each person. It was great. Everyone got something of his that he selected personally for them. And as he said, no one could squabble over his belongings after he died.

~~~

We had to cook his turkey at the neighbor's house so the smell will not make him sicker. Family members are bringing the rest of the food.

He has been in his hospital bed for so long, I doubt he will go outside for the picnic. There are lots of people to celebrate with him. That makes him happy.

Wow I can't believe my eyes. Two guys are carrying him out the front door. He is trying to eat turkey. He has had no solid food for many weeks. Now he is throwing up in the flower bed. Everyone is so thrilled that he tried.

People are commenting on how different he looks. Looking close, you can see his baby-blues still look kind-of like him, just more ancient, and sunken. One thing, this "Labor Day/Thanksgiving/Christmas" day will be remembered by everyone for years to come.

~~~

Excerpts from:

FLETCHER FAMILY NEWS Vol. 4
GRANDPA UPDATE

Garry is continuing to get weaker daily. He enjoys the family and other visitors, but the noise of the children gets on his nerves quickly. One of his newest sayings is "even his bones hurt." Some relief comes with the morphine inhalant treatment and patches.

~~~

Every time I remind him about coloring his beard, he keeps saying that he is "too tired" and "can I do it tomorrow?"

Even with a large family, it is difficult making sure someone can be here while I am at work. The kids all have children, jobs, and homes of their own that keep them busy. I discovered sitters for dying adults are available through hospice and their wonderful volunteers.

~~~

Sick again, I take him to the hospital. They admitted him and gave him a blood transfusion. This is the second transfusion so far. When he is stabilized, they will let him go home. He doesn't want to be here. He states unequivocally he doesn't want to die in the hospital.

~~~

Garry will not let the home healthcare lady change his clothes or even wash his face, let alone give him a bath. She is a very petite young lady. He has always been a very private and self-reliant person.

He doesn't like me bathing him either. I can barely get him into the shower, even with the rails and seat that hospice gave us. His legs are very long, and he has no strength to help me.

~~~

Family and friends are good about coming to visit. They bring meals, cards and love. One young man, years ago, had 'adopted' Garry and me as his second set of parents. He comes over and reads the Bible to Garry. One time he asked what passage he wanted to hear. Looking at me, he said, "You know.".

My response was, "Yes, the one about Hezekiah." He responded by telling the scripture reference for it, II Kings: chapter 20.

Since getting sick, he keeps talking about this story. Hezekiah was sick and asked God for more time. God told him he could have fifteen more years. I wonder if Garry is asking God for more time. I think he is hoping for those fifteen years, but with his medical training, he knows better.

~~~

So much company every night, I wondered if it was wearing him out. He had almost no patience with the kids. He was always great with them before he got sick.

One day, he got angry with one of them, and I saw him clenching his fists. The little three-year-old boy had done nothing wrong. I knew the pain of this prolonged illness caused Garry's behavior, because he would never have acted like that normally.

He got mad at me one day too. I was trying to put his T-shirt on him headfirst. I didn't think about the fact that he always did it arms first. Maybe I never even knew that. At this point is hard to tell.

He drew his hand back, and I thought he was going to slap me, but he didn't. Did he realize what he was doing so he stopped himself, or did he not have the strength to carry through with the action? I just know it is hard to see my husband in an act so foreign to his normal self.

~~~

Our adult Sunday school came to the house on September eighth for their class. Garry even sat up in bed. He felt it was an especially kind act. He missed going to church.

~~~

When I came home for lunch in mid-September, I found him on the floor in the bathroom. The hospice volunteer was an old friend of his. Garry told him to help him to the toilet, so he did. Garry then tried getting up by himself and fell. His legs are not strong enough to hold him.

The man ran to the bathroom and couldn't pick him up. Just then, the phone rang. It was our son calling from work to check on his dad. The man told him what had happened.

Moments after I arrived, he got there and carried his dad back to bed. I called the hospice emergency number. The nurse came and checked him out. He had at least one broken rib, but there was nothing that could be done for it.

~~~

Garry keeps telling me I am giving him the wrong medication and that I am trying to poison him. It is the illness; he doesn't realize that the doctor had changed the prescription or the dosage.

One day, he made me call the nurse back out so he could talk to her because he did not believe me. One drug that he is on is morphine. I think that either that or the pain makes him delirious.

~~~

Now he thinks I am hiding things from him. I have been publishing the family newsletter every few weeks since June. He told one daughter that I don't even show him the newsletters any more because I don't want him to know what I am writing about him. She knows I read each of them to him before I mail them out to everyone.

~~~

One thing I won't ever forget is Garry saying repeatedly that he had to go to the bathroom. He had on an adult diaper. He kept insisting and saying, "Why can't I go to the bathroom?" I tried to explain that I could not lift him.

Finally, I gave in. I put him in the wheel chair and wheeled him to the bathroom door. I was trying to hold him up, get him to the stool, and get the diaper off. He was having diarrhea all over. I sat him down and he slid off.

Tugging and pulling, I got him up off the floor. His legs were in the way when I tried to get him placed on the shower seat. He slid off, right into the tub. I kept saying, "I'm sorry, Hon," over and over. I got the shower seat out and got him comfortable in the tub and gave him a bath. By then, I was worn out. Again! (This seems to be an ongoing problem with me lately.)

Lifting him out of the tub was impossible. I couldn't do it. He only weighed about a hundred pounds but I still couldn't do it. He was embarrassed, so I let the water out and placed a towel over him. I called one of my sons-in-law.

He rushed over, picked him up, and got him back to bed. They were both embarrassed, but I didn't know what else to do. I am so thankful that I have family willing to drop everything and come to my aid at a moment's notice.

~~~

It's been a while since I went to church because I didn't want to leave him. Hospice staff held a church service at the house on September fifteenth. Several friends and relatives came. Garry couldn't sit up, but he was glad to be in a worship service with friends and family.

It pleased him that we brought church to him since he couldn't go to it. It was a great experience for everyone. Sometimes it's necessary to take church out of the buildings and into the community.

~~~

People do the weirdest things when sick, things they would never do otherwise. Garry is no exception. He picks at his clothes like there is something on them he is trying to remove. He tried to pluck the flowers off the bed sheet.

It brought to mind when my dad was in the hospital. He was hallucinating. He seemed to fold an imaginary shirt. It is strange to watch and try to figure out what they are attempting to do.

The best thing to do is play along as if it is perfectly normal. People who take care of dementia and Alzheimer patients probably have to do this.

~~~

A friend rang the doorbell and stuck a bag of takeout Chinese at me. She said that she loved us, and then she said goodbye. Impressive. That was one of the most thought provoking things anyone had done. There was no action necessary, not anything. I did not have to entertain her. The only thing to do was say thank you. Her kindness was greatly appreciated because I didn't have the energy to be hospitable.

This act of kindness is something I have told many people about. Most of us don't know what to do when someone is not their normal self because of circumstances they have no control over.

My advice, do an unexpected act of kindness. Sit and hold the hand of a sick or dying person, a family member in distress or a friend in a spiritual battle. Don't worry about your words. Just listen to their words, or their silence, or their tears.

In the book of Job it says that his friends sat with him for seven days before they said anything. Platitudes are not for someone grieving and truth may not be what they are yet ready to hear. Your silence can give more comfort than words they are unable or unwilling to hear. Then, when they are ready, pray with them.

CHAPTER 5

FINAL DAYS

Monday, the sixteenth of September, I went home on my lunch break. I was sitting in the rocker, watching Garry. He stopped breathing, started again. Then stopped again, over and over. I called hospice emergency line then called my work. I told them I didn't know when, or if, I could come back. They were very kind. They told me I had a job waiting when I was ready to come back.

The nurse came to the house and examined him. She explained it was usual for someone who was dying to stop and start breathing. I was afraid, none-the-less.

~~~

When we moved into this house, I had hooked up an intercom system beside his bed so I could hear him at night. I had it set loud, so that anywhere in the house I heard every breath that he took. I found it difficult to sleep that way, but I could not sleep at all unless I could hear him.

~~~

Garry doesn't know it, but coloring his beard is on the agenda today. It took me two hours to get it finished. I was trying so hard not to disturb him.

He slept right through the whole thing. Now, his beard is so dark that his hair looks even whiter and his skin looks so very pale.

Add that to the fact that he is now smaller than I am. He weighs about ninety pounds. He is so close to death. I know he will have an eternal body when Jesus comes to take us home with Him. A good thing, because there isn't much left of his earthly one.

~~~

Mom and the kids kept telling me to leave the house. I couldn't go, even though they would stay here with him. I couldn't bear to leave his side. What if I'm not here when he needs me, like in Michigan when the doctor's call told him cancer?

~~~

Today is Thursday, September twenty-sixth. It's his birthday. I think about last year, before he started chemo treatments. Our lives have changed so much.

His family came from Illinois, and the kids were in and out all day. He realized something special was happening. When told that it was his fifty-fifth birthday, he let out a holler that brought everyone in the house running.

We were all shocked. His voice had been just a whisper for so long. He seemed to regain his big, deep, booming voice, if only for a moment. It was long enough for us to know that he appreciated our efforts.

Remembering stories of other people waking from comas and being full of life just before Jesus takes' them home should have prepared me for what was to come. Maybe it would have been a little easier to get through, if I had realized. Even so, God always supplied my needs.

~~~

His sister stayed with me for a while. She used to be a nurse. It is helpful and comforting to have her here. She is a morning person, and I have always gotten my best sleep in the morning, so we worked out a compromise for my sleep problem. I will stay up at night with him, and she will relieve me in the early morning hours. It will work well.

~~~

Sunday morning, September twenty-ninth, Garry's brother and mother went back home. I went to church, since his sister was with him. Besides, I had to go because they played the tape he had written.

Yes, he wrote that sermon. It took him several weeks. He could only spend a few minutes at a time.

Of course, it was about Hezekiah. Garry said that God did not give him the fifteen years that He gave Hezekiah, but He gave him enough time to get his house in order. The title of the sermon was "Get Your House in Order."

Leaving was difficult for me, even with his sister sitting beside him. It was the first time I had been outside in so long. It was necessary for me to go, since he could not be there himself.

~~~

The church bulletin covers had a picture of sunflowers, the state flower of Kansas, on them. No way anyone knew, but while we were in Michigan, the sunflower had become Garry's favorite flower, but God knew.

It is very disturbing listening to my husband's taped sermon knowing what he went through to make it. The PA system was turned full blast to get enough volume to hear his voice. I remember his big, hefty, loud voice and hear that small, weak voice, and know he is home in bed, so very sick.

~~~

Home from church, I found Garry was not doing well. He was bleeding rectally. His coloring was wrong. There was purple on his legs, feet, and hands. I knew it was one of the signs his body's systems were shutting down. It had been coming and going all last week.

His sister and I kept washing up the blood and putting clean clothes on him. The minister came to visit. He tried to talk to him, but Garry was unresponsive. I started smelling the blood again. He left, so we could give Garry a sponge bath.

Mom went home for a while. I had done the dishes. His sister was sitting with him. She walked to the kitchen, saying she was going outside for a while and I should be with him.

While talking to him, I told him how much I love him and how good a father he has been and how grateful I was to have been his wife for these twenty-plus years. Then I told him it was okay to 'let go'. The kids are grown, and with God's help, all of us would make it through this.

My prayer was for God to please take him home, away from all the suffering and pain. I was holding his hand while praying. Even though my eyes were closed, I felt his spirit leave his body. Without opening my eyes, I knew he was dead. I thanked God for answering my prayer.

It was 3:30 p.m. Looking up, I saw one of my kids driving up, and his sister coming in the front door. She had asked me to sit with him because, from her time as a nurse, she knew death was eminent. Those last moments were so special. They will be mine for the rest of my life. A better gift could not be given.

~~~

Phone calls to hospice and my mom were done by me. His sister called their mom and brother. They had arrived back at their home, now they had to turn around and drive the ten hours back for a funeral.

Mom started calling family. His doctor called me and gave her condolences. The hospice caseworker, nurse, chaplain, and everyone else showed up. Both church pastors came back again.

Mom could not reach one of my daughters, but moments later, she drove up with her family. She was shocked, angry and upset because they had gone to lunch and not stopped here first so she could say goodbye.

It was better that way. God knew I needed alone time with him, and her family needed a meal before they got hit with his death. It wouldn't have been good for the young ones to be here.

When the funeral home came, all the children who lived in town were there, along with several friends. God is so very good.

~~~

It is just about 4:00 p.m. Attendants covered his body and are taking him out. I will remember this day forever, but I know that with God's help, I will be all right.

~~~

Then, suddenly, nothing feels right. Lord, what is happening? I can't breathe. The air won't come. I'm gasping. I now know where my soul resides in my body—it is in the middle of my chest, just below the collarbone. It feels like it is being ripped out. I have often heard about a marriage making two people one; I even agreed with that statement. After all, it says it in the Bible.

People also talk about love growing. I know now that when it grows, it puts its roots deep into your very being. When it leaves, those roots don't want to come loose; they are holding on for dear life. I feel that my breath and soul are trying to go with my husband. The hurt is so strong .

~~~

They are trying to take him away. I can't let them until I hold him once more. I uncovered his face and held him close. Someone tried to pull me away; I think it was my mom. She didn't understand that I just had to say goodbye one more time.

Stop! I must be strong for my family. This will be the end of my crying. It must be.

~~~

Excerpts from:

FLETCHER FAMILY NEWS Vol. 5

Garry is no longer racked by the "Pain of Cancer." He is being held in the arms of Jesus, in a land where there is no sickness or pain. Jesus Himself has wiped away all his tears. Garry is enjoying the rewards of having turned his life over to God. His work here on earth is being affirmed by his compensations there. I know he is enjoying every minute while awaiting our arrival.

~~~

The kids from out-of-town all flew in. Garry's son helped me with all the little things that needed done. Things like the handicap parking permit, insurance company, and a million other things I didn't even think about.

At the funeral home, I only had to tell them how many copies of the death certificate I wanted and pick the memorial folder. Garry had done everything else. He fulfilled his promise to make this go easily for me.

CHAPTER 6

GOOD-BYES

The license plate on our car expires today, September 30. When I went to get it renewed, the teller said she needed Garry's signature. I told her he had died yesterday. They told me they could not let me register the car without a release of his name on the loan from the bank. I am lost and upset.

We went to the bank, and they wrote a letter saying that his name could be removed from the title. Then it's back to the court house again.

The car has a vanity license plate that Garry had surprised me with. It reads, "I DEKR8." Now they are telling me I can't keep my tags. I need new ones because they listed our names with "and" between them instead of and/or. This is 'a word to the wise' for the future.

The crying starts. It doesn't want to stop. Back at the car I'm still carrying on. Now I have to take my husband's gift of the personalized license plate off the car and replace it with a generic one. All this the day after his death.

What do I do now? I don't want to go home, so Garry's son is taking me to get a cherry-limeade. I wonder why I want that (Yeah, right?)

Going home is frightful, so now he is driving me to Catholic Social Service. I want to talk to Sister Jane Albert for a while. She has been a good friend for years. More than once, she has helped me work through decisions or problems.

~~~

Back at the house, a truck was pulling off. Garry's sister had arranged the pickup of the hospital bed and all the other medical paraphernalia. She wanted it done while I was gone, so I would not have to see it. She is so very considerate. Few people would have thought about the pain that would come from seeing it happen. Her thoughtfulness is another thing that I will never forget.

~~~

Two days after Garry's death and all the kids are here. We are going through his wallet and personal papers. There was a picture of the family picnic this summer. He looks so sick. I feel like I am going to pass out from seeing it and remembering.

Everyone has been a big help. They have made all the business calls that were necessary. I didn't do any of it. Garry would be proud of them . . . and me, because I allowed someone else to do something for me.

Remembering when I did those things for my mom, I'm glad I could help her. I am glad that they are helping me now.

~~~

A large family and lots of friends are a blessing. They keep the house full of noise and love. The constantness (That may not be a proper word, but it does fit) of well-wishers is difficult.

Sometimes I take one person into the bedroom, kitchen or outside in order to have some quiet one-on-one time. Last night, Monday, the 30th, about ten o'clock, everyone had left but my mom and one of my daughters. I asked those two to leave. They were reluctant until I explained to them I needed to be alone.

After they left, I was alone with the quiet. It felt great. I could feel and just be, without having to be considerate of other people or worry about hurting their feelings.

Next, I cleaned the kitchen, stored food people had brought by, and watched my soaps (I have been taping them for years.) Then I picked out my clothes and jewelry for the wake and funeral. I will wear the long black dress that I wore when we got married. Yes, there's a great story behind that too. Going to bed, I read my Bible, as usual.

~~~

At 8:15 a.m. the next morning, the funeral director called for some logistics about the obituary notice. There is a cost per inch to have it put in the area newspapers. That surprised me. I had always thought that the papers printed them as a public service. It shows what I know, or maybe how time changes things.

~~~

Walking through the house, I expect to see someone here. Closing the door to the bathroom, I realize I didn't have to. No one else is here. All alone for the first time in my life, I may never have to close a door for privacy again.

~~~

The droplets of water in the bathroom sink seem to be happy. They are "dancing" in the light. That reminds me of the clock that our youngest daughter gave us for Christmas when he first got sick. It chimes a different song each hour. Garry used to dance to those chimes every hour.

He took the batteries out of the clock. He couldn't stand to hear it and not be able to dance. Garry must be dancing in Heaven now. The water droplets were God's way of showing me that.

~~~

The trash has to go out for pickup. There are ten bags. They stink because of all the bloody diapers. Blood and death have a strange stench about them.

It is very hard to carry the bags. The smell of the blood overwhelms me. A couple of days ago, this was a part of my husband's physical body. These bags, hold a part of him, and I have to take them to the curb.

~~~

It seems there are too many memories most days, but I am worried that my memories of him may dissipate if I don't keep them fresh in my mind.

Will I be able to remember songs he changed the words to? Like "It's beginning to look a lot like Easter," or "Lady in red I adore you, pull down your pants, I'll explore you." Or his greeting of, "How is my beautiful, sexy, good looking, white woman I married twenty years ago doing?"

~~~

The wake on Tuesday night went well. I was a perfect hostess. There were no tears from me. Garry would not want me unhappy. I kept the facade on the outside so no one would know what I felt on the inside. I wonder how many times people have fake fronts, so their emotions don't come tumbling out.

~~~

The funeral is today. I walked into the church to find the casket in the entry, not the chapel. It upset me beyond reason. My soul cried out. He needed to be at the front of the chapel. I told the funeral attendants to move him, or I would do it myself.

I was rude, obviously I am not taking this as well as I thought. Anger seems to be one of my ways of dealing with grief.

In my mind is a picture of the way it must have been at his friend's funeral in this same chapel last year. He also died of cancer. Garry wanted to come but was too sick even then.

~~~

They lay Garry out in his Salvation Army uniform in his casket, with the guardian angel pin from our neighbors in Michigan on his lapel. After the service, I took the pin for myself to remember this time and how God got me through.

The funeral was perfect. Military honor guards lined the walk as the people entered. The ushers assisted people to the few remaining empty seats. The chapel looked great with flowers, flags, and an open casket. Inside the top of the casket that Garry had selected were the words, "Coming Home." That was so appropriate.

During the service, people could speak about him. There were so many wonderful tributes. Our pastor from Michigan did the eulogy. The message from my pastor was what Garry would have wanted.

There was even a part where Garry himself spoke. Yes, unknown to me, when he taped his "Get Your House in Order" sermon, he also taped a goodbye to be played at the funeral. It started, "Hi, Donna..."

He tried to think of everything, but one thing he did not think through was how surprising and difficult hearing his voice, with no warning, would be to me and everyone else. He had made the pastor promise not to tell anyone.

~~~

Looking back, I don't know anything else I could have done for Garry. I have nothing to regret. It is important to know that I did everything possible.

My husband felt the same way because he did all he could by preparing and planning everything possible for me. He talked with the funeral home staff, picked out the program covers for his funeral service, and even planned for the congregation to sing "Victory in Jesus."

The song to be sung by our son was selected by him too. He tried to sing it, but was too emotional to sing.

~~~

October second was a beautiful autumn day. The Leavenworth National Cemetery service had full military honors. When the flag was presented to me, I gave it to Garry's mother. I had not planned to do that; it seemed to be the right thing to do. They gave me three bullet casings from the 21-gun salute. I gave those to his three biological children. When the guns went off, it gave me shivers. Everyone jumped, including me. But it was even worse when the trumpeter started playing "Taps." That's when the tears started flowing, not just mine, but everyone's around me.

Afterward we went to the fellowship hall at the church. I believe it is important to share an informal time of caring and remembering. Ladies from several churches had dinner for all of us. The women worked hard to make sure everything was perfect, meeting all our needs. There were lots of people to share memories with. No one wanted to leave and end all the stories shared around those tables.

CHAPTER 7

LIFE AFTER DEATH

The house seems so strange. There are lots of friends and family around, but it seems so empty. The hospital bed, oxygen tanks, condenser, and medical supplies are all gone. So is my husband.

Today is Thursday the third and my in-laws are leaving. I don't want to say goodbye. How do I tell his sister how much she has helped me?

The sympathy cards are too much for me. I open them, see who they are from, take out memorial gifts, and put them in a basket with the newspaper article, death certificates, and book from the funeral home in it. When will I have the strength? It's too hard now.

In coloring Garry's beard, I now realize, I was preparing his body for burial, another Bible ritual. God was preparing both Garry and me.

~~~

Friday, the fourth, the last out-of-town guests left. I decided I had to rearrange the furniture in the house. There is a big hole where the hospital bed had been.

Some of the kids and I went shopping and bought bookshelves. The kids put them together for me. When I tried to move a stack of records, I found I couldn't straighten up my back. I had broken it by falling on ice a few years ago. The doctor said that it was stress and ordered some medicine.

~~~

Everyone keeps popping in, checking on me. Sometimes it irritates me, because I have always been very independent, but mostly I like it.

Mom and I went through the house, a room each day, sorting Garry's things. They went in boxes in the living room. When people come over, they take what they want. This is a different, but good way to handle things. Garry would approve.

~~~

His retirement check goes to the bank on the first of each month. I paid our monthly bills, but the government took the money back out of the account, which caused the checks to bounce.

He was not living the last day of the month, so I could not keep the money. It was his, not mine. My widow's benefits on his retirement will not start for two or three months. The insurance check is due in about ten weeks.

~~~

Today is Sunday again. One twin is sick, so I went with them to the hospital. I find I keep looking at the clock and remembering what happened last Sunday.

Each click of the clock brings a distinct memory of what happened last week. Three-thirty in the afternoon was the time he died. It's three-thirty. And here I am in the emergency room.

~~~

Eight days since his death, I am going back to work. They promised they would keep my job for me, and they did.

What am I going to do at lunch? Every day since I started working here, I have been spending lunchtime at home with my husband. I went to the church office to see mom.

~~~

Almost two weeks have gone by. It is now October eleventh. I got takeout for lunch today. I can't get up the courage to eat in a restaurant by myself. The guy who gave me my order asked how Garry was doing. He has known him for twenty-five years, but he did not know that he had died. It was a difficult situation, both for him and for me.

It seems impossible to me that the world just keeps going. Life as I have known it has been brought to such an abrupt stop. How can anyone not know that he is no longer here? Don't they know that nothing is the same for me?

~~~

During the first song at the evening church service, I felt like my head was going to explode. Two weeks ago, my husband died. I feel strange. I am having trouble breathing, and noises hurt my ears. This morning, the PA system volume was lowered for me, yet the sound hurts my head.

Mom is taking me to the hospital. I don't know if I am sick or in grief. The doctor says it doesn't matter which it is, I am being admitted.

~~~

I left the hospital on Saturday. I went to the cemetery. There was mud everywhere. I literally 'walked out of my shoes'; the mud was so bad.

At Garry's grave, I had to stick my hand in about a foot of water to pull the temporary marker out to read it. His grave had sunk in and the water was standing on it. I started making a trench with my hands for the water to get out. I kept saying, "Garry, I'm sorry," over and over. It reminded me of the scene in the bathroom. I was saying the same thing, again.

Angry, I went to see the caretaker. He saw how upset I was about the grave condition. I told him it was no way to run a national cemetery. He assured me it would be taken care of. Again, anger seems to be my shield. Previously, I had thought that I was a slow-to-anger person.

Grief makes a person do things out of character to their normal personality.

~~~

It feels good to be home and to go back to work. They have shown me so much kindness, even though I walked out on them, stayed home with Garry, then was in the hospital for a week. They certainly did not have to give me my job back.

~~~

Allergic to one prescription I bought when I got out of the hospital and no money to buy the replacement medication. I went to The Salvation Army office and got a voucher for the new medication, which was very embarrassing. A few years ago, I was giving out vouchers from that very office. Now I was receiving one.

This was a very humbling experience. Humility is something very difficult to learn. If I allow it, God can teach me yet.

~~~

October twenty-fifth, my forty-eighth birthday, I got a call about a job in a different town. The position is a little more than two hours away. It would be in the office. I tell him I am sick and in mourning. He said he knew that, but he still wants me to come. Again, I tried to decline. Then he said that his new wife is a friend of mine. When I heard her name, I knew this was where I needed to be. I am going for the job interview.

I don't know what to do. I got a call about a job at the church headquarters in another state. Asking God to show me, I did something completely out of character, a Biblical "fleece." Opening my Bible five times, all the passages pointed me to the first job offer. Mom will lend me money to move since I have none.

~~~

Looking in my closet, I realized I had been wearing all dark colors since Garry's death. He would not approve, since I have always preferred to dress in red. A move means new beginnings. It is time for me to stop wearing mourning colors all the time.

~~~

God has provided for me again. At the end of October, I receive two widows' benefit checks, and I also got the insurance check. I was glad I didn't have to wait as long as they said. Mom got her money back. I paid off the medical bills and funeral expenses and will have money for my move.

~~~

The landlord is giving me problems. He says that I have a lease and I have to pay the balance or he will sue me. I got the lease out and showed him the clause that I requested he add to it. It stated if my job took me to another location, they had to free me from the lease. He is not happy. But I am glad I knew about the little legal item.

~~~

Some of the kids and their families helped me move. The twin's family liked the area. Now they want to move in. I told them to give me two weeks to get myself set up, then they could come and join me.

Well, they came and stayed… husband, wife, and three kids. It wasn't that they wanted to move, but they didn't want me to be alone. This seems to be a standing theme with my family. God has certainly blessed me.

~~~

Holidays have always been big at our house. What will I do with myself this first Christmas without Garry?

The problem is solved. I am going to Mexico with my mom, my eldest, and her daughter. My daughter planned it; she is so thoughtful. She doesn't want me alone this first Christmas and New Year's.

~~~

After some time, the kids had not moved, so I did. I moved two blocks away. I believed I was ready to be on my own.

While unpacking, I found one of my husband's Salvation Army uniforms. I was beyond shocked. They buried him in his uniform. Of course, I realized it was not the same one, but knowing didn't take away the pain or tears. I had forgotten about this one.

~~~

Another grandson was born. My daughter was pregnant with him when her daddy died. She named him Garrett Wayne, after his two grandfathers. I called him "Baby."

My daughter confided she had a difficult time calling him Garry for a long time. I told her I had the same problem.

Starting in middle school, he asked to be called Garrett. He has allowed me to continue calling him Garry. It was hard to call him Garrett, and even harder to call him Garry. I finally got over that. It is getting easier for all of us now.

He is a very sweet young man. He has his grandpa's disposition. He is a kind soul, and I tell him he lives up to his namesake very well.

~~~

I am stopped in my tracks when I run into little things that belonged to my husband. I gave the uniform and one of his shirts that I found to a new church member.

~~~

My youngest daughter moved in with me. That was nice; it was just she and I. All the family has been worrying about me being alone again since I moved. Maybe everyone will stop worrying, but somehow I doubt that.

~~~

Reliving the days before Garry died is a regular thing. I wonder what they did with the T-shirt he had on when he died. It was one of mine. He couldn't wear his own because he weighed less than eighty pounds at the end.

What if I had waited until he died to color his beard for him like I thought I would? There is no way I could have done that. Whatever made me think I could?

~~~

Easter Sunday, was one of the hardest days since he died. Remember that uniform I found? The man I gave it to wore it for his church enrollment. Alterations were unnecessary. He even has a full dark beard too. This is a little too scary for me.

The whole day was strangely full of memories. I remembered the Easter when we attended his sister's church enrollment. His illness and the way he handled it brought that "heathen sister" to God. She has become a living tribute to the life that he led.

The solo I sang that morning was one of Garry's favorite songs. The breakfast brought back memories of Easter's past and many shared meals, the 'Son-rise Service' without him standing beside me . . . And so many other things.

There were other memories, like him setting the table each morning for me. He would put out a bowl and spoon, along with a glass of ice water, a jug of milk, a napkin, two kinds of cold cereal, and my Bible. He wanted me to start my day right, both for my body and my soul.

~~~

Sick again. I went to the doctor for a sinus infection and said "By the way I have a pain in my side." I ended up getting my appendix out.

~~~

Grief counseling was suggested. The lady in charge was very kind. She told me I needed to cry. That is hard, because I promised myself that I wouldn't. Why do we put stock in being so strong and not showing emotions?

Jesus showed us about grief at Lazarus' grave. John 11:33-36, "When Jesus saw her weeping, and the Jews who had come along with her also weeping, He was deeply moved in spirit and troubled. 'Where have you laid him?' He asked. 'Come and see, Lord', they replied. Jesus wept. Then the Jews said, 'See how He loved him."

"Jesus cried." Not for Lazarus, because He knew He would raise him. But because the people were crying. He feels our pain and grieves with us. This is an amazing revelation.

CHAPTER 8

MEMORIAL WINDOWS

The Garrett W. Fletcher Stained Glass Memorial Windows were dedicated today. The memorial service was great. There were sixty-three people there. One of our daughters told her story of her dad. The words of three ministers honored him. All three had worked with him in three different locations. About twenty people told how he had touched their lives.

Our son did an excellent job when he sang his solo. The song was the one Garry had picked to be sung at his funeral. Although unable to sing it at the funeral, it was a great tribute at the memorial. He has a beautiful voice and has performed lots of times at many events, starting in high school. He has sung on TV a couple of times.

The windows are gorgeous. They are just like he planned, a lion and a lamb lying down together. Both represent Jesus, the Lion of Judah and the Lamb slain for the world.

Peace ... It will come for me. I get a preview of the peace of Heaven just looking at the windows and knowing that he is already at peace with no more pain.

~~~

"I Never Knew Garry When," Written by a friend after the dedication.

"I had a good friend who died before Garry. She had known him before Donna. She couldn't believe the difference she saw in him when she met him again here at church."

"Because of Garry we have something beautiful to see as we come in the front door, a scene that should remind us of what God can do for us."

"I was given the opportunity to see the stain glass windows as they were being made. They completed one, but the second was lots of little pieces of glass laying on the table. It reminded me of the Gaither song:"

> "Something Beautiful"
> "Something beautiful,
> something good,
> All my confusion.
> He understood.
> All I had to offer Him
> was brokenness and strife,
> But He made something beautiful of my life."

"I am so glad and I praise God that Garry allowed the Lord to make something beautiful of his life."

Her letter reminded me that when Jesus makes the changes, He makes us better than we can be on our own. It's His love shining through us.

CHAPTER 9

DEALING WITH GRIEF

An offer came to get my job in Michigan back, but I turned it down. I love the people, but there are too many hard memories. Besides, I need to be closer to my family.

~~~

Well, my youngest daughter has moved out, and the eldest, (the one who planned our Mexico trip) is moving in along with her daughter. It is nice to hear a child's laughter in my home again.

~~~

A skit about a man in a wheel chair caused me to cry again. His son was asking when he was going to try walking again.

Leaving the room was my only option, because all I was hearing was my husband saying, "But why can't I walk?" and "Why won't you take me to the bathroom?"

I felt like the day he died, with the roots being pulled out again. But like that day, I had friends and family checking on me, encouraging and grieving with me. Still, I grieve even though he died six months ago. When will this grief be over?

~~~

Sometimes I get very lonely. I plan things in my head to tell him when I get home, like I have always done. I wonder if other people do that?

Going to the grocery store is depressing because he always enjoyed shopping. I don't like cooking. He did that more than twenty years. Little things like polishing my shoes get me down because he took care of me in so many little ways, ways I didn't always realize.

Going to a restaurant by myself is unbearable. I miss him so much. He will always be in my heart. The little things hurt, reaching for him in my sleep, listening for him at the door, waiting for the phone to ring. All those little things are the tough, big things now.

~~~

It's the middle of May, seven and a half months since Garry died. Today I played our song over and over, John Denver's, "Lady, My Sweet Lady." The lyrics mean even more to me now.

> "Close your eyes and rest your weary mind.
> I promise I will stay right here beside you . . .
> I wish you could know how much

> I love you. Lady, my sweet lady,
> I'm as close as I can be . . ."

"As close as I can be." Only if he would still be with me, keeping that promise. He is as close as he can be, here in my heart and soul.

Still, I can't stop crying that same cry. I know that cry well now. Before my husband died, I had only heard it twice. Once, it was my cry when my first born was taken from me by her father. (Because of Garry's tenacity, she was returned.) The second time, was from my mother, the morning my dad died.

This is a whole body, mind, and soul cry. It comes from deep within, where most things never touch. It can't be stopped or held back. It is the lament of the heart. It is the cry that God gave us to cleanse our whole being so we can start fresh.

~~~

Dear God, I want to remember. Help me get through this grieving so I can remember without the hurt. I know I will never quit missing or loving him. But I know that with Your help it will get easier. Thank You for the years, laughter and tears, and all the children You gave us to share. We had a wonderful life. You supplied all our needs every day. Thank You for all that You have done for me. But, right now, I thank You, Most Awesome Lord, for grief and the cleansing it brings. AMEN.

~~~

A job interview is taking me to Michigan, about an hour from where we had lived. I had to turn the job down. There were too many hard memories of his sickness while we lived in that state.

Another position in Kansas came open, only an hour away from home. I am serving as an assistant pastor again. I still miss Garry, sometimes I still cry.

~~~

Time for license plate renewal for my car again. I stood in the courthouse and cried because of the memories from last time I was there. They came flooding out, there was nothing I could do to stop the memories or the crying.

The clerk couldn't understand what was wrong with me. She kept asking if I wanted water or what she could do for me. What she did was hold my hands and care.

Yes, she could have walked away. Just like in the Good Samaritan story. Instead, she, and the Samaritan both did all they could for a person in pain. People, even strangers, many times amaze me.

~~~

The sympathy cards are still unread. They are waiting in that same basket. Someday, maybe.

I use a pair of his gloves for driving. They are way too big for me. It helps me to feel that he is with me. I know he isn't, but the little things help.

Sunflowers are the decorations in my kitchen, in his memory. The centerpiece that is on the table is the brass basket of silk sunflowers that I bought for his funeral.

Going out to eat now is possible. I don't have to go alone. My mom is living with me. One day while she was visiting, I told her we should live together. It took her over three hours to make the one hour drive home that day because she was thinking about my proposition.

Her accepting has helped with a lot of things. We both have someone to talk to, and since we are widows, we understand and can commensurate with each other's grief.

Talking to Garry in my head is an everyday event for me. His picture hangs where I can see it from my bed. My love is just as strong as it ever was.

People must tire of hearing me, because I talk about him to anyone who will listen.

His family and I visited his grave once. It looked a lot better than last time. Now there is grass instead of standing water. He is not in the grave. He is happy in Heaven.

~~~

My female cycle is all messed up. I had three periods last year and two this year. The doctor tells me it is because of my husband's passing. That's okay. It's one less thing to deal with.

The multitude of silver hairs I have must be from the same thing. These are the true marks of widowhood.

~~~

One of my sisters made 'corner pouting dolls' for me to give the family for Christmas. I picked out the hair and clothes for each one.

The one for Garry's sister was very special. For a while, Garry had tried to hide his baldness with toupees. Problem was, he kept growing out of them as his bald spot got bigger and he would have to buy a larger one. So he decided to stop wearing them.

I took one of them and fixed it for her doll. I told her she could tell no one because they would be jealous. She treasures that doll. It has stood in the corner in her bedroom since then. And only she, her husband, and I know the story behind it.

~~~

Garry's gloves disappeared while I was working the Christmas distribution at church. They were on the table in front of me, then they "walked away." I was upset. I had everyone looking to see if they could find who had "picked them up."

Someone must have taken Garry's gloves. It is terrible to steal from a dead man. I know that's petty. The person who took them didn't know. They probably needed them more than I. I have more, maybe they had none. I need to quit holding on to material things.

~~~

Even through all the pain and grief, I thank You, God for the love Garry and I shared, and I pray You will allow me to find someone else. I don't enjoy being alone. You are such a wonderful God, knowing what I need before I do. You have been so gracious to me. I thank You, Lord, for the Your healing powers of grief. AMEN.

~~~

Christmastime four years after his death, I went through picture albums and gave the kids each some family pictures.

In January, I made a memory album for Garry's sister. I put in lots of pictures with captions, letters, cards, newspaper articles, his obituary, and his death certificate.

These came from that basket that I have been afraid to touch all these years. Yes, I decided that I could handle it. The Bible says in Ecclesiastes, "There is a time for everything.".

Everyone seeing the album loved it, so I made one for each of the kids. That was my Christmas project for that year.

~~~

The holidays, anniversary, his birthday, and death date are all still difficult to handle. Times like Mother's Day, Valentine's Day, and my birthday are hard too. With no gifts, special meals, cuddling and kisses, no anything.

Garry used to make up time-rhymes for me. Like; "It's 10:02, time for you" or "It's 12:20, need some money" or in the morning, "7:04, I'm out the door".

The clock that plays the music that Garry loved to dance to sits in a box in my garage. I still can't cope with the memories. The same daughter bought a new one for me. It plays children's nursery rhymes each hour. It still reminds me of the other clock and Garry dancing.

CHAPTER 10

DATING

Dating. I am doing it but I don't think I am fair to the gentlemen because it is very difficult to not compare them to Garry. I bring him up in conversation often. I hope it doesn't put them off. He is a big part of whom I am. But if it does, so be it.

~~~

One of my not so smart actions was an engagement. It was only for a short time before I broke it off. I was lowering my standards, and I knew it. Garry would not have approved.

The man was nice enough until I caught him cheating at pool with his son. He informed me I was never to correct him in front of anyone. If he said "the grass is red and the sky is green" I was to agree. That is not how I have ever lived or want to live.

I think it was a case of wanting to be close to someone, anyone. It was just too soon. I knew that too. But I definitely believe that God has another husband out there for me somewhere. The Bible says those widows under sixty should remarry.

~~~

Can I expect anyone to be as loving and kind as Garry was? But no matter how wonderful the guy is, I can't follow Garry's instructions. I will not give a new husband Garry's wedding ring.

Even through all the pain and grief, I thank God for the love Garry and I shared, and I still pray that God has someone else for me. I don't like being without a husband.

My memories of the life we shared will always be precious and cherished. The grief still comes, but it also goes. Sometimes it's rough, but the memories are sweet.

~~~

A trek to Illinois to visit my in-laws is still on my yearly calendar. They consider me part of their family, and it makes me feel good that they care. The kids and grand-kids are their link to Garry.

Surprise. I polished my shoes myself a few times so far. It is getting easier, and it is cheaper than giving them away and buying new ones.

Life is still going on. I know Garry would want me to be active and have fun. So I try. . . For myself and for him.

~~~

Dating has been interesting and disappointing. My expectations are high. There is a single's group here in town. I am uncomfortable going to the functions because I don't know anyone.

~~~

A couple of men on Match.com are interesting. One of them is Larry Everitt. He told me that his daughter in the Ozarks found my profile and said for him to check me out. He lives in Kansas City and I am back in Leavenworth. God had to have a hand in the logistics to make all that work out.

He is the sweetest guy. He has been a widower eight years. Only one problem. He is eleven years older than I am. He is also old-fashioned and a gentleman. He told me he wanted to court me. My response was, "You are too old for me. I already buried one husband and don't want to bury another one." He promised he would live to be a hundred.

My mom loves him. She told me to give him a chance because he can't be too bad since he retired from the Army as a Lieutenant Colonel.

He brings chocolates every time he comes to see me. I told him I don't need that much chocolate. Besides, I prefer M&Ms with almonds. So what did he do? He bought a case of them and every time I get in the car there's a package of M&Ms waiting for me.

CHAPTER 11

MOM

Mom has dialysis at six in the morning, three times a week. She refused to get up for me several times, so Larry started driving an hour each way to take her. He would say, "Betty, you need to get up now," and she did. But it never worked for me.

She talked to her kidney doctor about stopping dialysis. He said "If you stop, you will live two weeks then die." It was difficult, but there was no changing her mind when she made a decision.

My sisters were angry with me because I didn't force her to go to dialysis. But they didn't know how difficult it was getting her out of bed and dressed, then trying to keep her from pulling the needles out of her arm. Her doctor told me I had to accept her wishes. It wasn't easy, but I understood her pain and her decision.

She has never been one to show physical affection, even though I knew that she loved me. So it was very special that I spent the last two weeks of her life sitting or laying beside her in her bed. That was the closest time I had ever had with my mother. It was because she knew there was only had a short time for her to live.

About a week before she died, she asked me when I was getting married. Yes, Larry was that great guy. I told her we were planning a May wedding. She said that she didn't think she could wait that long.

A few days later, I asked her if she could keep a secret. She smiled, so I said, "I am getting married tomorrow." Yes, I lied. The wedding was still three months away. Her smile got wider, and she seemed to be contented. I think she wanted to make sure I had someone to take care of me. In addition, she likes Larry.

Two days later, I was on my way to a doctor's appointment while her other three daughters were at my house with her. They called me to come back home because she had died. She died two weeks to the day of stopping dialysis.

How would I have handled it if I had been there? I'm very glad I didn't have to find out. She had lived with me for six years. Her death left a hole in my heart, and my home was empty . . . Again.

~~~

The memory of Garry choosing presents, and how great that was, returns to my mind. The contrast I am seeing from mom's family is scary. Death can bring out the worst in people. Greed is a terrible thing.

Families get torn apart because of petty arguments over material things. I need to figure out a solution to this problem. I don't want this occurring when I die. Is it even possible to stop that kind of thing? This is a problem that can only be solved by Jesus.

CHAPTER 12

MOVING FORWARD

Larry and I got married. Garry's sister (that ex-heathen) was my maid-of-honor. All the kids, their spouses and young-uns were there. No, I did not give Larry the wedding ring from Garry.

~~~

After having been Donna Jean Fletcher for so long, I didn't want to change my name. Larry said that was fine, as long as I added his name to it. So I ended up with a hyphenated name.

~~~

Larry is a wonderful man. He even polishes my shoes for me, but only when I ask. Before we married, he asked me if I would like to retire and travel. That was an easy decision. I had to get a passport. Wow! We have gone to Europe several times. Poland, Germany, Austria, France, England and Switzerland are countries we visited.

When stationed in Germany, he met his first wife. When we go there, we visit her family and they have accepted me into their lives. It is wonderful.

~~~

Garry would approve of my choices and my life. I have forty-four grandchildren and sixteen great-grand-kids. In addition, through my current husband, two more children, four more grandchildren, spouses and two great-grandchildren added to my family. I'm happy and contented.

Thinking of Garry and Mom makes me smile . . . and sometimes I cry. But I have learned that God made tears to cleanse the body and heal the spirit . . . So it's okay.

~~~

God is helping me get better at handling death. I sat with a friend while she was dying. She told me she wanted me to be with her at the end and preach her funeral service. I did both. Of course, the memories of Garry came flooding back, even though it was going on eight years.

~~~

My father died about a week after being told that he had colon cancer. I was with him during that week. As I learned from the past, the most important thing that we can do is just be there.

After his death, I ended up in isolation at the hospital. This time, I had influenza A. The doctor says that I may have contracted it when I was at the VA hospital with my father. A family member's death, and hospitalization for me, seem to go hand in hand.

Debra Kelly

CHAPTER 13

DEBBIE

A shocking phone call just came from my eldest daughter, Debbie. How can this be? The doctors have diagnosed her with cancer. She is only forty years old. Four of her sisters and I head cross country to Virginia.

~~~

She looks so small. She has lost a lot of weight. The cancer is in the lining of her stomach. I have not been told, but as with Garry, I know she is terminal.

We spend this time shopping, remembering, talking, cooking, eating, playing games, and singing. We did all the things we love to do together.

After a while, her sisters went home. I told her "I am staying until you tire of me and kick me out." She seemed pleased with that response. I am blessed. My new husband, Larry, encourages me to do whatever is needed to take care of her and her family.

Debbie always told me she would take care of me when I got old and frail. Now I am helping her. Life is not fair. I need to remember what it says in Isaiah 41:10; "So do not fear, for I am with you; do not be dismayed, for I am your God. I will strengthen you and help you; I will uphold you with My righteous right Hand."

~~~

Twelve and a half years since Garry died and the memories are upon me again. I think of each family member and wonder how they are going to handle this. How can we go through it yet again?

Doctors' appointments and hospital visits are all familiar, but these feelings are so different. This is my child. How can this be happening to her? She has a married son; a teenage daughter; and two boys, seven and almost five. Her husband lost his job by the company downsizing several months ago. That allows him to be with her, but I still ask, how unfair is all of this?

Her daughter left today for a summer job at the church camp in Kansas City. She did not want to go, but Debbie insisted.

~~~

Debbie is going to have chemotherapy after her stomach is removed. We went to the American Cancer Society to check out their free wig program because, as we know too well, she will lose all her hair. We got a cute one that looks just like her own hair.

~~~

The surgery is over. She has tubes going in and out of her body. She will be unable to eat for a long time, then only through a feeding tube. Eventually, she may eat actual food, but only a few bites at a time.

~~~

A week after her surgery, she got out of ICU. Two days later, she got the tube out of her throat, so she could talk to us again.

They took the tube out, but her voice was tiny. So what did she do? She checked on someone from her church who was in the hospital, too. She was always caring for other people.

Her husband and I took turns staying with her or with the boys at home. I had stayed with her that evening and left about 10:00 p.m.

At midnight, we got a phone call saying she was back in ICU. She aspirated on the acids from her belly. She was in a coma. Why didn't I stay later so I could have been there? Maybe I could have helped her.

How many times in our lives do we dwell on the "what ifs?" I know it doesn't help and it can't change anything. Everyone gets the "what ifs" syndrome at some time. We have to be careful that we don't allow it to take over. God is in charge. We can't change what has happened in the past. We can only learn and move forward.

~~~

The people from her church prepared meals for us every day. They held a prayer meeting in the ICU waiting room for her. There were about forty people there. Afterward, the oncologist told us she would not make it through the night, but she surprised us all.

She had been in a coma, with moments of awareness. Today she recognized her eldest son's voice when he spoke to her. When I told her that her husband had accepted Christ into his life last night, she grabbed my hand and squeezed! She had been praying for him for almost twenty years. God answered her prayers. Again, God used an illness to bring a loved one to Him.

My prayer for her was the same as it was for Garry; that God would take her soon and not allow her to suffer anymore. The doctors and hospital staff were wonderful. If they thought of something, anything, that just might help her . . . they tried it.

So many tubes going in and out of her, I couldn't count them all. She was so bloated that her skin crinkled and cracked when touched. It was like wax paper.

But none of the things they tried helped. I wished they would just leave her alone and allow her to die with dignity. I kept telling myself that she would be pleased, knowing that someone else's life could be saved because of what the hospital staff learned from all they were trying to do for her. But it was still hard.

~~~

She lived for two more days. I called one of my daughters and had her go to the church camp. Two of her sons, Debbie's daughter, and another of my grandsons were working there for the summer. She pulled them aside to tell them what had happened. Before she had even gotten finished, there were campers and staff coming in crying, giving hugs and prayers.

Larry bought tickets for the two of them to fly back to the funeral. We ended up having two funerals, one in Virginia and one in Kansas. They buried her with military honors because she served in the Navy.

Her brother recorded himself singing "Angels Among Us." We played it at the funeral. He wanted to sing live, but was sure that it would prove too emotional. He had learned from his dad's funeral. I bet he never wants to sing at another family funeral ever again.

~~~

Now I know what my mother-in-law felt like when my husband died. It is beyond words; it is indeed indescribable. A child should never, ever, ever die before their parents! Since it happened to my child, I understand it more than I would ever have wanted to.

What is worse? Losing a spouse or a child, I don't know. I just know that no one can fully understand the pain of either until it happens to them.

~~~

A DVD of her life is my gift to each member of the family. It shows pictures of her from birth through the 21-gun salute at her funeral. Her brother's song is on it and also Alan Jackson singing "Sissy's Song":

> "Why did she have to go?
> Lovely, sweet young woman,
> daughter, wife and mother.
> She flew up to heaven
> on the wings of angels.
> She walks with Jesus.
> She's smiling, saying,
> 'Don't worry about me'."

That song may be called "Sissy's Song," but it tells of Debbie's life. We played it at her funeral in Kansas.

We often obtain spiritual growth during the roughest times. I must keep on the right path to see her again. God is taking care of her and all my other loved ones. One of these days, I will be "going home."

~~~

Two months have passed. I am still in shock, and feel unbelief and grief. Debbie's husband returned to Virginia with the kids. They will go to a public school for the first time, since Debbie is no longer there to home-school.

If only. . . I wish they could stay here with us, but I understand them going back. They have lost so much. They need the home that she made for them.

The wig from the American Cancer Society was taken to a free clinic. She would want it for someone in need. It still had the tags on it, since it had never been used.

~~~

Children and pets pick up on our feelings and what we are thinking, even when we say nothing. A three-year-old grandson asked me if I was sad when his Aunt Debbie died. He told me he was sad and that he cried. Then he asked me why she died and how she got to Heaven. How did he know Debbie was the reason that tears were streaming down my cheeks?

His next question was even harder. He asked me when Grandpa Larry and I were going to die. What do you say to a child?

His questions reminded me of my Last Will and Testament. I had to rewrite it. Debbie was the executor. I never dreamed that she might die before me. God used a three-year-old to tell me what I need to do.

~~~

It was a couple of months before I could read the condolence cards that I got this time.

My home seemed so empty and quiet without her and her children there. They have spent summers with me for years. That summer just dragged on and on. I had no energy and no desire to accomplish anything.

When I emptied my suitcase, I found a Mother's Day card in it. This is the last card I will ever get with my daughters' signatures on it. Even during her illness, Debbie had bought a card and had her sisters sign it before her surgery. The verse on it read;

> Mothers and Daughters are Gifts to each other for Life
> Mothers and daughters have a bond of closeness that will never break,
> A friendship that's unconditional between two never-ending friends,
> Mothers and daughters are closer than any two best friends.
> One is always looking up to the other,
> And both are looking out for the other.
> They are perfect listeners, helpers, advisers, hopers,
> Honesty brokers, promise keepers, and dream sharers,
> The love between them is proof of love's power.
> And she signed it, "Thank you for all you have done. We love you."

"Gifts to each other for Life" . . . I am grateful for the gift God gave to me of her life. And the gift she gave me of her love, four grand children plus a simple little thing like a Last Mother's Day card.

A thank you, especially one with such perfect timing is rare. I have been blessed beyond measure again and again. The blessings fill my cup to the top and overflowing.

~~~

More blessings abound. Debbie's daughter came to live with Larry and me while she attends college.

After her mom's death, she had to go to public school. Her mother had told her she would be a senior in the fall. But the school said that she was a junior, because of her age. Her dad stood up for her and got them to test her for placement. I was so proud of him. She passed all the tests with flying colors, as I knew she would.

~~~

When we tried to enroll her in one of the state universities, they said she would have to pay out-of-state tuition, which was extravagantly higher than state residents. I explained that her mother had died, and she was now living with me. It did not matter. The school could not enroll her without receipt of the higher tuition and fees.

They allowed her and one of her cousins to be a part of the marching band for the football games that year. The two of them enjoyed that. She ended up attending the community college.

~~~

God has blessed me so abundantly by allowing me to be a part of my granddaughter's path to adulthood. I am amazed, watching her as she grows and matures, attending classes and working.

A job was offered to her when a local restaurant owner needed help. She refused the waitress job because of her shyness. She became the hostess. The owner took her under her wing and worked with her. She ended up not only as a waitress but as the manager of a new restaurant.

That young girl is no longer shy. She has blossomed into a fun, exciting and very capable young woman. She has a great job, lives on her own and takes cross country road trips by herself, just like her mother did.

Larry E. Everitt

CHAPTER 14

LARRY

My life is full and happy. My new marriage is better than I could imagine. Larry is so wonderful. God has indeed blessed me with a strong and loving man.

~~~

He sold his house, I rented mine out, and we bought one in the country. It has almost two acres and a beautiful large Koi fish pond. We do a yearly third of July party in the backyard. A couple hundred people show up. There is a grill, and tons of food, a fire pit, s-mores, waterslide, bouncy house and fireworks. Some of my friends even provide live music. It is the highlight of the year.

~~~

Easter egg hunts for the grand-kids in the spring and hay rides and chili suppers in the fall are more glorious memories.

~~~

Christmas is almost unbelievable, with all the food, cider, hot chocolate and desserts. Everyone has a present under the tree. Then each person goes to the 'gift room' and selects something for themselves. There are over a hundred unique items to choose from. There is a room for kids too. It is fun to have everyone here together.

~~~

Larry bought me a dog. He is a Puggle, a mix of Pug and Beagle. This dog loves everyone, and everyone loves him. Noone can come in without petting him.

At first, I wasn't sure if I could like him or not. His eyes bulge out, his ears look like a bat in flight, and his bottom teeth stick out, making me think of a vampire.

But I looked beyond the facial features and quickly fell in love. (Just like with people, sometimes we have to look past the outside.) He was the first dog that I ever allowed to sleep in my bed.

We got him from Safe Harbor, a program run by the state prison. Prisoners take abandoned and neglected dogs and keep them with them 24/7, love them and train them, then they are then put up for adoption.

We had him for four wonderful years, then he got sick. He is in pain and will not make it, with Cushing's disease and two blockages in his bowels.

We had him cremated then did a funeral in the back yard. Lots of friends and family came. Each of us told a special memory of him. Everyone had the chance to help dig the hole and bury him. The service ended with a surprise from Larry. He had a fireworks fountain shaped like a fire hydrant to shoot off. What a sendoff for a great pug. This dog was a cherished family member. Fireworks at his funeral were a special culmination of the family funerals we have had.

~~~

Larry takes me shopping for clothes often. He has the cashier put a chair by the counter so he can sit and talk to her while I pick out clothes. I bring them to the register and he looks at them to see if he likes them or not. He says if he doesn't like something, I can still have it. I just have to pay for it myself. But that scenario has never happened. He always buys whatever I pick out.

~~~

For my sixty-fifth birthday, we went to a movie and dinner. Before dinner, he took me clothes shopping and to a new little boutique that sells Swarovski Crystal jewelry. One of his daughters had told him she thought I might like it.

On one of our Europian trips, I had visited a very large Swarovski Jewelry store. While he was in woodcarving classes, I often took off shopping and sightseeing in Austria and Germany, either by myself or with other wives I met there.

Well, we are in this store. He told me to pick out something I liked. Very quietly I asked if he was aware how expensive this brand was. He said "don't worry about it." After finding a pair of earrings, he said, "pick out a necklace to go with them."

Without speaking, I showed him the price tag on the earrings. Words would be heard by the workers. It was a tiny store. His comment was "It's your birthday, and it's only money." So we found a necklace that matched the earrings.

He must not have looked at the price tag. When the cashier told him the total, he yelled, "What?" I whispered, "I tried to tell you." The cashier and her assistant stood with their jaws hanging down, not knowing what to do. After a very pregnant pause, he said, "Okay, go ahead, she's worth it". I was very glad we were the only ones in the place.

Needless to say, I cherish that jewelry. Not because of the extravagant cost, but the wonderful story behind it and the love he shows every day.

~~~

At all the restaurants in town, he is known as the Ink Pen Man. Ink pens with his name, phone number and the statement, "Wanna Trade?" on them are given out for the exceptional service he always receives. He calls everyone by name and remembers everything about them. I wish I could have a small portion of his memory.

He says he has about 10,000 ink pens from all over the world in his collection. He probably does, since they are everywhere. Baskets, cups, boxes and multiple dresser drawers are full of them.

~~~

One thing we enjoyed doing was reinstating the Outhouse races for Buffalo Bill Days. Larry likes to talk, so he talked everyone into volunteering. We did it for several years, then turned it over to a younger person.

~~~

Larry calls himself a computer widower because of all the time I spend in my office on the computer while working on this book. But really, he encourages me in my writing.

~~~

There are so many grand-kids I can't keep track of them. I know there are well over forty now. I even have sixteen great-grand-kids. God's blessings keep flowing. I praise Him for His goodness to me and for holding me up through the rough times.

~~~

My new car and has my old vanity plates "I DEKR8". Another one of those blessings.

~~~

Larry has lots of saying that he comes up with. The family calls them Larry-isms. Like:

"The proper name for underwear is Seat Covers."
"Getting old is better that the alternative..."
"Peculiar, Missouri, what a strange place. Rather peculiar."
"I went to Fair Play, Missouri and they just didn't play fair at all."
"I'm so poor I can't even pay attention."

"If you heard this before, it's ok because I would rather tell you twice than forget to tell you."

Or:

"Eggs are to be served Stomped and Run over."
"Six of one or half a dozen of the other."
"My name is Larry, guess you know yours."
"First, let's relax for a minute."
"Is your shirt cotton or felt." (As he grabs at it).
"Yes, even a blind squirrel finds and acorn once in a while."

When someone says "Hey, Larry," the response is always "My name is not Hey, hay is for horses."

And the Larry-ism he uses on me all the time. He spells out R.. E. .L.. A.. X one letter at a time when he wants me to sit down and rest. A very hard thing for me to do as a type A personality. Most of the time now, I sit down before he gets to E.

He has no problem relaxing, just give him a Harlequin romance or a cowboy book or turn on a Hallmark movie. Make it a Christmas Hallmark movie and he will be thrilled. That is his favorite relaxing time.

~~~

His mom got his name from a cowboy book she was reading when he was born. Therefore, he is always emphatic that his name is Larry, not Lawrence, because there are no cowboys named Lawrence.

~~~

Larry has three hobbies, photography, amateur radio and woodcarving. They have published his photography all over, in newspapers, magazines, calendars, and even phone books. He tells new photographers not to do weddings or babies because it is hard to please women, but that never stops him.

~~~

Everyone prizes his woodcarvings, since he doesn't sell them. He gives them to organizations to auction as money makers or just gives them away. They are on display all over, like the pharmacy on Ft. Leavenworth, the local Feed Store and even the Driver's license bureau.

One of the things he likes to do is inform beginner woodcarvers to tell their spouses it is okay for them to carve in the house because wood chips are messy but clean, nothing dirty about them.

~~~

Larry teaches all three of his hobbies to kids and adults. He believes in sharing. When teaching woodcarving, he always places a box of band-aides on the table. He says it's a reminder to pay attention and carve away from yourself.

He uses Morse Code and his amateur radio knowledge as a member of the County Emergency Readiness team.

~~~

We are very active and volunteer in different groups and events around the area. Being retired is not boring, we are always busy. I enjoy this life, traveling whenever and wherever you want and doing what you want, when you want.

~~~

"1-800-call-Larry" is his code name in town. He teaches everyone how to use their electronic stuff. He has classes for basic computer skills for groups of seniors. Phones, printers and computers are toted in. He repairs them and explains how to use them. If they can't bring them in, he even makes house calls. He never charges for his work. It is his way of sharing God's gifts.

~~~

We have had several kids and grand-kids come and stay with us for extended periods of times. Even one of Garry's kids lived with us for a couple of years. Larry is such a fantastic man and so accepting of all my family and he considers each one's needs.

CHAPTER 15

CHANGES

Larry has developed congestive heart failure. Even though he is on oxygen all the time, he is still teaching classes, judging 4-H and doing woodcarving demonstrations at schools in the four surrounding counties.

~~~

He believes in my Mom's advice about the aches and pains of illness and old age. "You are going to hurt, no matter where you are, so you might as well go and enjoy yourself."

~~~

Larry, like Garry, always enjoys shopping, so he shops for me. Now he uses those run-away electric carts to get around. But that does not slow him down at all. He has Tonto by his side so he can keep going. Tonto is what he calls his portable oxygen. He likes all that cowboy stuff.

~~~

His schedule is now a little less full. He sleeps in a recliner in our bedroom because he can't lay down flat.

Before going to sleep, from across the room, I hear him singing "Good night, my love, pleasant dreams and sleep tight my love." He has so much love to share.

~~~

The doctors have put him on hospice, after several extended stays in the hospital, to pull water out of his body. Larry said he liked Garry's idea of a farewell "Shindig", but he wants to have a "Bon Voyage" party. Very appropriate for Larry, the world traveler.

We held it on December twenty-first. With the use of the internet we planned it in less than a week. The editor of the local newspaper did a front-page article about Larry and volunteerism. He included the information about the party.

It was a great turnout and everyone's comments were basically the same. They couldn't believe he was on Hospice, because he looked great and his wonderful personality still overflowed. Of course, he made sure everyone got an ink pen from his collection to take home with them.

E-mails and cards from all over the world came from those unable to attend. Afterward, he said he did not know the impact he had on so many people's lives. It was wonderful people were able to tell him those things and make his last days so special.

~~~

The biggest problem he had was not being able to do his volunteering or shopping.

He said he was not in pain and did not understand why he was on hospice. He figured he had at least another year to live. The next week he decided that maybe he only had a couple of months. Because of my experiences, I felt he only had a few days.

~~~

He was himself until the last two days of his life. Then he started seeing people that weren't there. He asked me "what are those two guys doing over there?" and "what is that lady talking about?". The next evening, he wanted to know why I "let that man change his clothes in our house".

He was having trouble breathing, so I gave him his second dose of morphine. His body was shutting down.

~~~

Three in the morning I laid down. I was so tired. I didn't want to sleep, but I did anyway. When I woke, he was on the floor after falling out of the recliner. No longer would he need the oxygen or walker. He was with Jesus.

~~~

Like when Garry died, people were there immediately. One of his daughter lives a half hour away, yet she and her husband were there before the ambulance. Family willing to drop everything at a moments notice, even at 5:30 on a Sunday morning is great.

(A new realization, both of my husbands died on a Sunday. I don't know what that means, but it is a strange coincidence.)

~~~

We all went to I-Hop to celebrate his life in his favorite restaurant. He would have liked that. One waitress followed me into the bathroom to tell me how Larry had listened to her problems and gave her encouragement every time he saw her.

~~~

The twenty-two days after his "Bon Voyage" party were spent with his daughters and their families, friends and all of my family, all talking with him. He loved to talk.

When anyone came over, he would tell me to give them a woodcarving or a personal item.

~~~

The afternoon of his wake there was an ice storm. I thought no one could come, but I was wrong. The Patriot Honor guard were there. They helped people park cars and get into the building. We gave away ink pens to everyone.

~~~

He wanted to be buried at Fort Leavenworth. He had served served almost thirty years in the Army. But the cemetery is full so they are only taking cremated remains. We had an open casket funeral at church because he wanted to be laid out in his uniform.

Pictures and woodcarvings were on display. And guess what? We had ink pens for everyone as a special Larry remembrance. He would have loved that.

Afterward, there were full military honors in the parking lot with the gun salute and taps. Because of the ice and cold weather, with all doors open, we watched from inside the church.

~~~

That 10,000 ink pens got sorted and taken to local schools, restaurants and other organizations. He definitely was not exaggerating about how many he owned.

~~~

After the cremation, the ground was frozen solid. We had to wait till spring for his burial.

COVID-19 had set in so we ended up doing a small service several months later. Again there were military honors from the Patriot Guard. Taps sounded out. That is the most difficult thing at a military funeral. That trumpet, so soulful, brought back memories of Debbie and Garry too.

~~~

One of his daughters helped me walk through the mirage of red tape with the military to get my finances in order. She was defiantly a God send for me. It was easier for me this time. I kind of knew what to expect.

~~~

Listening to my mother was the best thing I did. She told me to give Larry a chance. He didn't live to be 100 as he said, but I got fifteen wonderful years with a fantastic man. God has blessed me more that I ever dreamed possible.

~~~

People from the different groups we belonged to came and took things their group could use. The Ham Radio club, the wood workers guild, woodcarvers, Carousel Museum, Bible Study, Artist group, family and friends helped get things organized for the estate sale. Garry's son came and helped sort out electric and hand tools. I needed the help because I didn't even know what some of them were.

~~~

The estate sale was a success. It brought in enough to pay the movers, with some left. The day after the sale, people were scheduled to come remove the left-overs. Only one big problem. That was March 16, 2020. The first day of lock-down for COVID-19.

Since, the house had to be ready for the market in two weeks, many people came to my rescue. We put the fire pit to use, burning everything we could. This was necessary because the antique and thrift stores were all closed. And everyone was ordered to stay in their homes.

This was the hardest day of my life. Burning memories and furniture and things that would normally be donated. I felt my life going up in that fire. My body felt weak. It felt like my bones were melting, like the Wizard of Oz bad witch. One of my widow friends stood beside me at the fire pit and literally held me up, physically, mentally, emotionally and spiritually.

She called a man who owns a junk business. He brought a couple more men. They took everything that could not burn. They even came back and cleaned out the fire pit.

Another widow lady painted the inside of the house for me. She refused payment for her services. She would not even allow me to buy a meal for her. We were not close before, but ended up being great friends. We shared many meals on my patio during the lock-down. When the restaurants re-opened, we started going to lunch a couple times a week. We also go to Bible Study together.

We have lots of things in common. Like the fact that her late husband was named Larry. God brings people to you when you need them the most. What more could I want?

~~~

The virtual tours of the house panned out. We sold it twice. The first one was an Army officer. He had to back out because the Army changed his orders.

CHAPTER 16

MOVING ON

One of my daughters and her husband helped me by allowing me to build a mother-in-law's suite in their basement. There is a private entrance, driveway and parking, a fenced yard with a patio and a flower garden.

The widow who painted my house is a wonderful flower garden person. She took me to the local nursery and helped me select flowers. Then she had to teach me how to tend them.

One bush has white flowers with red centers. They are the size of a saucer. They close at night and reopen in the morning. What are they called? I can't remember. I just enjoy them. Maybe they are hibiscus, but I don't know.

~~~

I definitely would not get the amenities I have here in an apartment downtown. Plus her family does all the yard work and maintenance.

Anytime I want, they share meals, TV time, evenings of board games and lots of love. A grandson brings me baked goods hot from the oven. A granddaughter brings Taco Bell, and I get drinks from Sonic from my son-in-law. My daughter provides transportation and help with my medical needs. This is part of the beautiful life that God has blessed me with in moving here.

~~~

Larry helped me with the floor plan and deciding what furniture I would take with me. It is a lot bigger than I would have expected, inside and out. We have a shared laundry and storage room, plus an art room, since my daughter and I are both artists. We enjoy doing all kinds of things together.

It was fun to plan the apartment, from the layout, to appliances, cabinets, colors and everything in between. I have decorated lots of houses but I never got to plan one from the ground up. There is even a doggie door for my four-legged friend.

~~~

A new silver blue sectional has hobnails, and it is tufted with jewels. I even put blue jewel knobs on the cabinet doors. This place is definitely me, top to bottom.

~~~

Two of the ladies that helped me clear out the house attend church with me. We have started a weekly prayer group with the three of us. They are also widows.

In all this, God brought together a group of widows who have become close friends. They were in my circle of acquaintances before, but we were not close. Now, I don't know how I got by without their friendships.

~~~

One of my daughters brought meals to Larry and I when he was sick. She continues to bring them to me now that I have moved. These are the things that make me feel so loved.

~~~

Larry's cousin called me and asked if I would take a river cruise with her in Europe. She is also a widow.

We had a great time. We went to the Netherlands, Germany, Switzerland, France and Italy. To sit on a boat and watch God's beautiful nature, and centuries of human history go lazily by is an amazing thing to experience. Tasting the different cultures foods, walking the cobblestones, touring the churches and castles, shopping for regional specialities and meeting the different peoples are things that make me understand how much diversity God has provided for us.

~~~

My life has always been good. I have had few reasons to complain. Yet, I have never had so many people help me and bless me in so many ways as now. It is so humbling, yet so amazing.

~~~

Now, when I think of loved ones who passed on, I remember what is says in Isaiah 57:1-2; "The righteous perish, and no one takes it to heart; the devout are taken away, and no one understands that the righteous are taken away to be spared from evil. Those who walk uprightly enter into peace; they find rest as they lie in death." They are at rest. I strive to live my life so I will be worthy.

CHAPTER 17

MEMORIES

Before we got married, I had asked Larry if I could keep my last name since I have been Donna Jean Fletcher for so many years. He said "Sure, if you add my name to it." Two last names are confusing. People never know what to call me. Doctors' offices can't find my records because they get the names mixed up. To simplify things I am changing back to one last name.

~~~

Keeping with family tradition, there is now a great-grand baby named Grant Everitt, after Larry. My children, and now my grandchildren, are so thoughtful in carrying on the names of special family members who have passed on to Glory.

~~~

A corner in my bedroom has a sign that reads; "Our Story". One of my daughters gave it to me. The wall has pictures of family members, past and present. There is also a table of memorabilia.

It gives everyone a chance to remember and gives the young ones a glimpse into our family history.

~~~

Sometimes, we don't appreciated what we have until it's gone. I have found that memories, pictures, memorabilia and talking about loved ones helps to ease the pain and encourage the happy thoughts. Memories can be a 'good' hurt. Like cold ice cream going down a sore throat.

My life is full of happiness and contentment. The valleys and hard times of life make us appreciate each of the hilltop experiences even more.

Memories is a word that I have used a lot in this book. I think they are something very special that God gives us to remember and learn from. Memories can be great, frightening, sad, happy, funny, painful or comforting, just to name a few. Sometimes they can be all these at once. They are the mind's picture book, complete with smells, voices and emotions.

Memories are from the mind and heart. They are each one a jewel that God has given. We can polish those jewels and cherish them or we can store them in the deepest, dark recesses of our minds. These jewels of life are to be shared. Just like Swarovski jewelry, if we don't get them out, polish them up and use them, they will tarnish.

~~~

Paul stated in Philippians 4:12-15, "I know what it is to be in need, and I know what it is to have plenty. I have learned the secret of being content in any and every situation, whether well fed or hungry, whether living in plenty or in want. I can do all this through Him who gives me strength. Yet it was good of you to share in my troubles."

These are words I am trying to live by. Instead of being self-sufficient as I have always tried to be, I want to accept help from others with grace, become more God-centered and content, no matter what my circumstances.

~~~

Lord, I thank You for giving me the ability to write this book and for allowing me to share my hurt and my happiness with others, that through reading it they might become closer to You.

Thank You for the physical, emotional and spiritual healing You have and will continue to give me. Thank You for new and old friends who supported me every step of the way through this journey.

Thank You for my family who share this glorious life You gave me, both the pain and the happiness.

I am blessed more and more each day. I know I don't deserve all the wonderful memories You have given me, but I thank you so much for them, and all the joy that you give me every day of my life. AMEN.

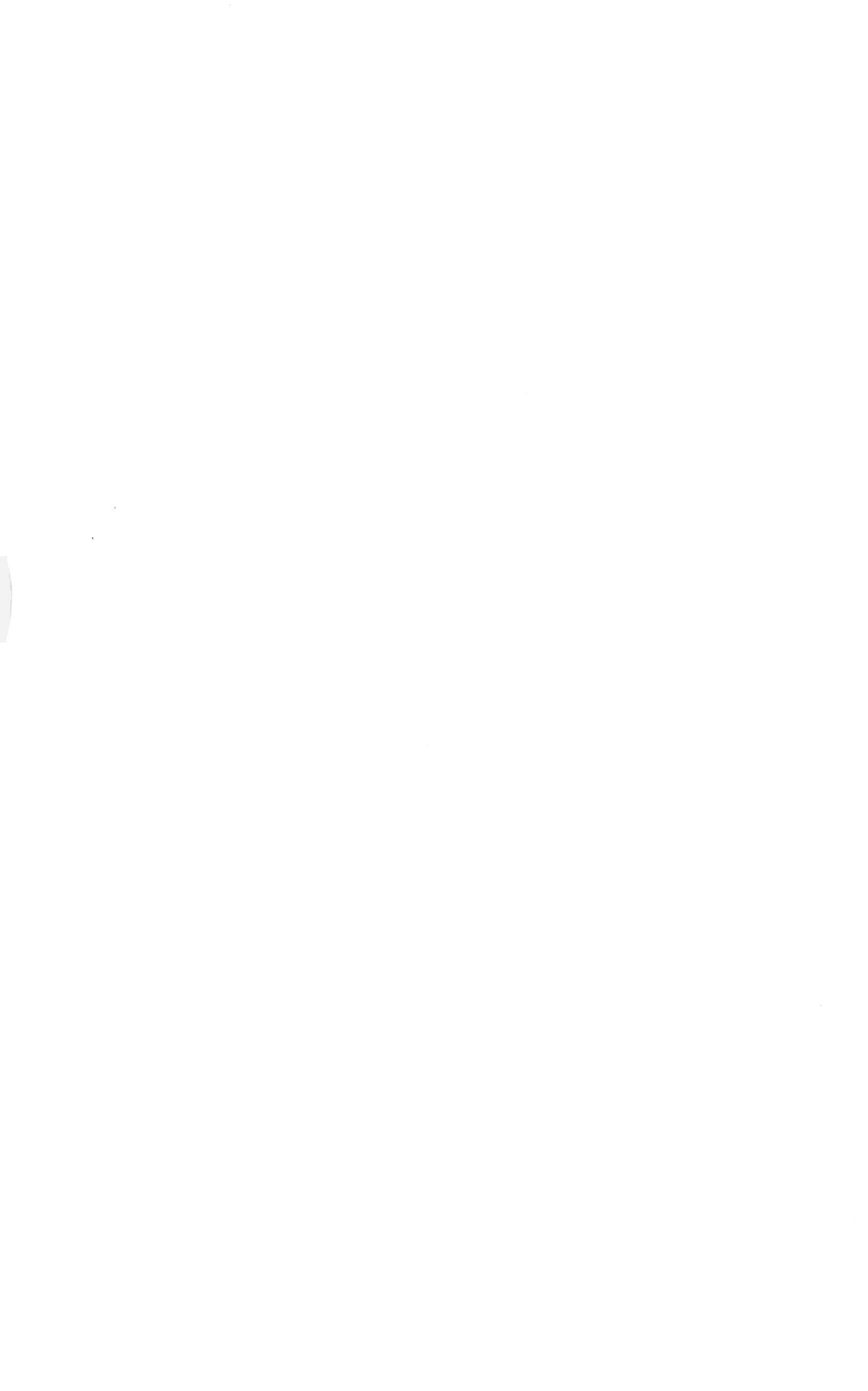

"He will once again
fill your mouth with laughter
and your lips with shouts of joy."

Job 8:21

www.ingramcontent.com/pod-product-compliance
Lightning Source LLC
Chambersburg PA
CBHW060401080526
44583CB00012B/419